AF585271

AUSTRALIAN LANDSCAPES

FORESTS
IN AUSTRALIA

RACHEL DIXON

REDBACK publishing

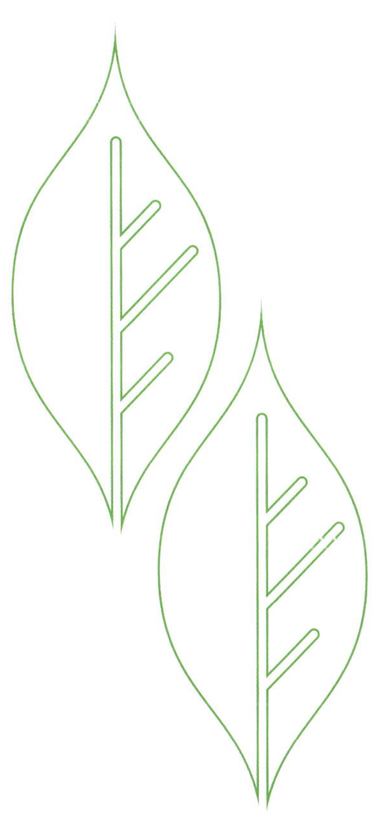

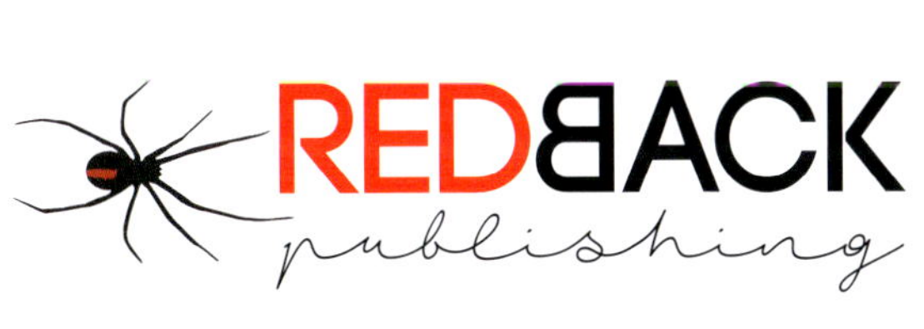

First published 2018 by
Redback Publishing
PO Box 357 Frenchs Forest NSW 2086
Australia

ISBN 978-1-925630-21-3

Author: Rachel Dixon
Editor: Jane Hinchey
Original illustrations © Redback Publishing 2018
Originated by Redback Publishing
Printed and bound in China by Leo Paper

Acknowledgements:
Abbreviations: l—left, r—right, b—bottom, t—top, c—centre, m—middle
We would like to thank the following for permission to reproduce photographs: p10m, p11 State Library of Victoria, p15t National Library of Australia - PIC Solander Box A27 #R4718-Forest with native camp & mia mia's, 1851, p16b Poyt448, p17m butupa, p19t Sputnikcccp and p21 Atamari via wikimedia

Cataloguing-in-Publication details are available from the National Library of Australia

Contents

What is a Forest?

In Australia, the Department of Agriculture defines a forest as having trees at least two metres high and with a leafy crown covering at least 20 per cent of the land surface. This means that some sparsely treed areas in Australia are stilll called forests.

There are many different types of forests based on the dominant kind of trees in them. Each forest grows in one or more of these three ways:

Woodland Forest

leafy crown covers 20% - 50% of the land surface

Open Forest

leafy crown covers 50% - 80% of the land surface

Closed Forest

leafy crown covers 80% - 100% of the land surface

Differences in forests and their ecosystems are a result of many factors, including the underlying rocks, soil depth, climate, water and the destructive effect of past fires.

Role of Forest Biomes

CARBON STORAGE - Carbon is one of the elements used by trees to grow. Because of this they store a large amount of the Earth's carbon. When wood is burned or decomposes, this carbon is released into the atmosphere as carbon dioxide, which is a greenhouse gas.

TOURISM - Forests are a source of income through tourism.

SPIRITUAL ROLE - Some forests are places of spiritual significance.

BEAUTY AND ART - The beauty of forests inspires human creativity.

HEALTH AND SCIENCE - Forests contain plants that are likely to be future sources of medicines and industrial chemicals.

WILDLIFE - Forest ecosystems support many plants and animals that cannot live anywhere else.

ECONOMIC ACTIVITY - Forests are logged for timber for building and for products such as pulp and woodchips. Most of the world's paper comes from forests.

FAST FACTS

- Australia has 125 million hectares of forests
- There are 2 million hectares of plantation forests
- Forests cover 16% of Australia's land area
- Australia has 3% of the world's forest area

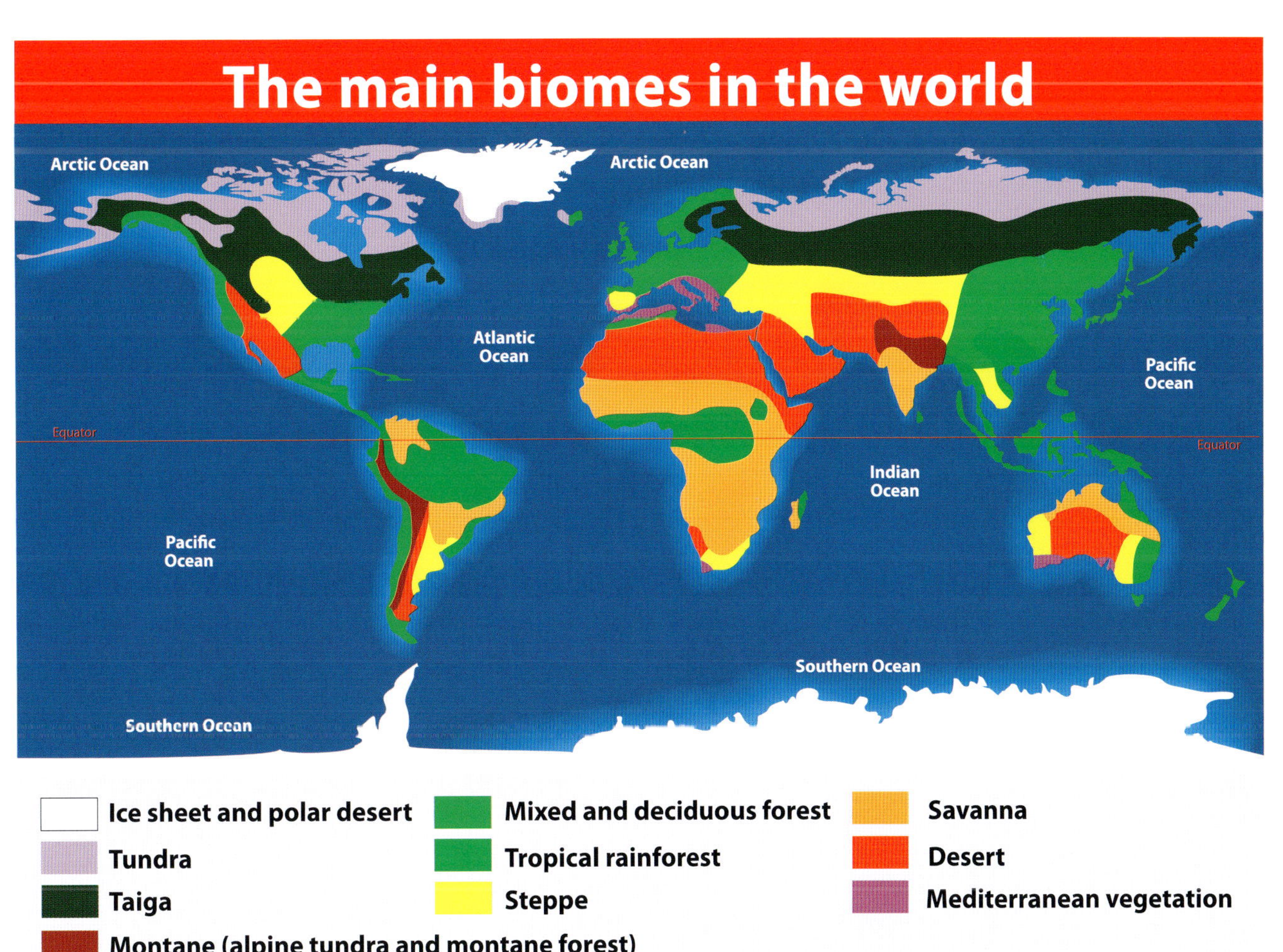

Threats to Forests

Extreme Weather

Weather events such as cyclones, droughts and floods can destroy whole forests. Cyclones tear apart or uproot trees and other vegetation. Floods drown trees and leave behind a layer of silt that smothers small plants. Long droughts can destroy forests and kill trees that are hundreds of years old.

Climate Change

Rising temperatures may result in the loss of forests in areas where the heat and lack of water would kill the trees. Warmer temperatures in frozen parts of the world could contribute to an increase in vegetation. However, the growth of trees and whole forests would take a very long time and would depend on a stable ecosystem developing.

Bushfires

Eucalypt forests can survive a bushfire since they have evolved ways of quickly regenerating after a fire has passed. Unlike eucalypt forests, rainforests and alpine forests cannot regenerate after a bushfire.

Housing

The need for land to house Australia's growing population is a threat to forests.

Agriculture

Consumer demand for food produced from crops and livestock is a threat to forests. The burning of rainforests by farmers in southeast Asian countries produces cleared land that is used for agriculture or to graze livestock. Plantations producing trees for palm oil are one of the most common uses for land claimed from rainforests in those countries. Palm oil is used in fast foods, confectionery and cosmetics. In Australia, early settlers cleared forests to produce the cities, suburbs, farms and country towns where we live today.

Plant Pests and Diseases

When forest vegetation is under threat from changes in the climate, rainfall or nearby deforestation, it is more likely to suffer from the effects of attack by pests and plant diseases.

Feral Animals and Weeds

Feral animals destroy plants growing on the forest floor by eating or trampling on them. Weeds invade the forests and take up water and soil nutrients, which stops native plants from growing.

Mining

Mining of resources usually requires the destruction of the forest to reach the minerals in the ground. Contaminated mining wastewater can destroy plants and animals that live nearby or even a long way downstream if a river is polluted by the waste.

FAST FACTS

- Europe is the continent with the largest proportion of forest cover
- Indonesia is losing its forests at one of the highest rates in the world
- Australia is still clearing land for agriculture and mining

Certification

Owners of forests in Australia can apply for certification to prove that sustainable forestry practices are being used. The Australian Forest Certification Scheme can certify that any products from the forest have been produced in a sustainable way and have been legally harvested. This means that mass destruction of the plants and animals of the forest has not occurred to produce the resource being sold. Some of these forest products are timber, paper and food.

Sustainable forestry involves:
- Replanting with seedlings
- Careful use of chemicals
- Not taking trees from areas of cultural significance
- Converting to plantation forests only in small areas of the native forest

Montreal Process

In 1993, Australia was one of the nations that met in Montreal, Canada to discuss the future of the world's forests. The aim of this meeting was to ensure the conservation and sustainable management of forests around the world. The Montreal Process sets standards to assist nations to maintain their forests into the future.

Who Owns the Forests in Australia?

National Parks

Forests in national parks are owned by governments.

Plantations

Plantations are owned either by businesses or by the government, although they may be grown on land that is leased from the government.

Australian Aboriginal Land Councils

Local land councils have traditional ownership of the forests in their area.

Private Owners

Some forests are on privately owned land. Laws and regulations control the cutting down of trees or the clearing of these forests.

World Heritage Forests in Australia

UNESCO chooses World Heritage Sites based on their importance. They include buildings and places of cultural significance or natural beauty and rarity.

Gondwana Forests of Australia in New South Wales and Queensland - Many of the plants and trees in these forests have ancestors which grew on the ancient continent of Gondwana, which existed over 180 million years ago.

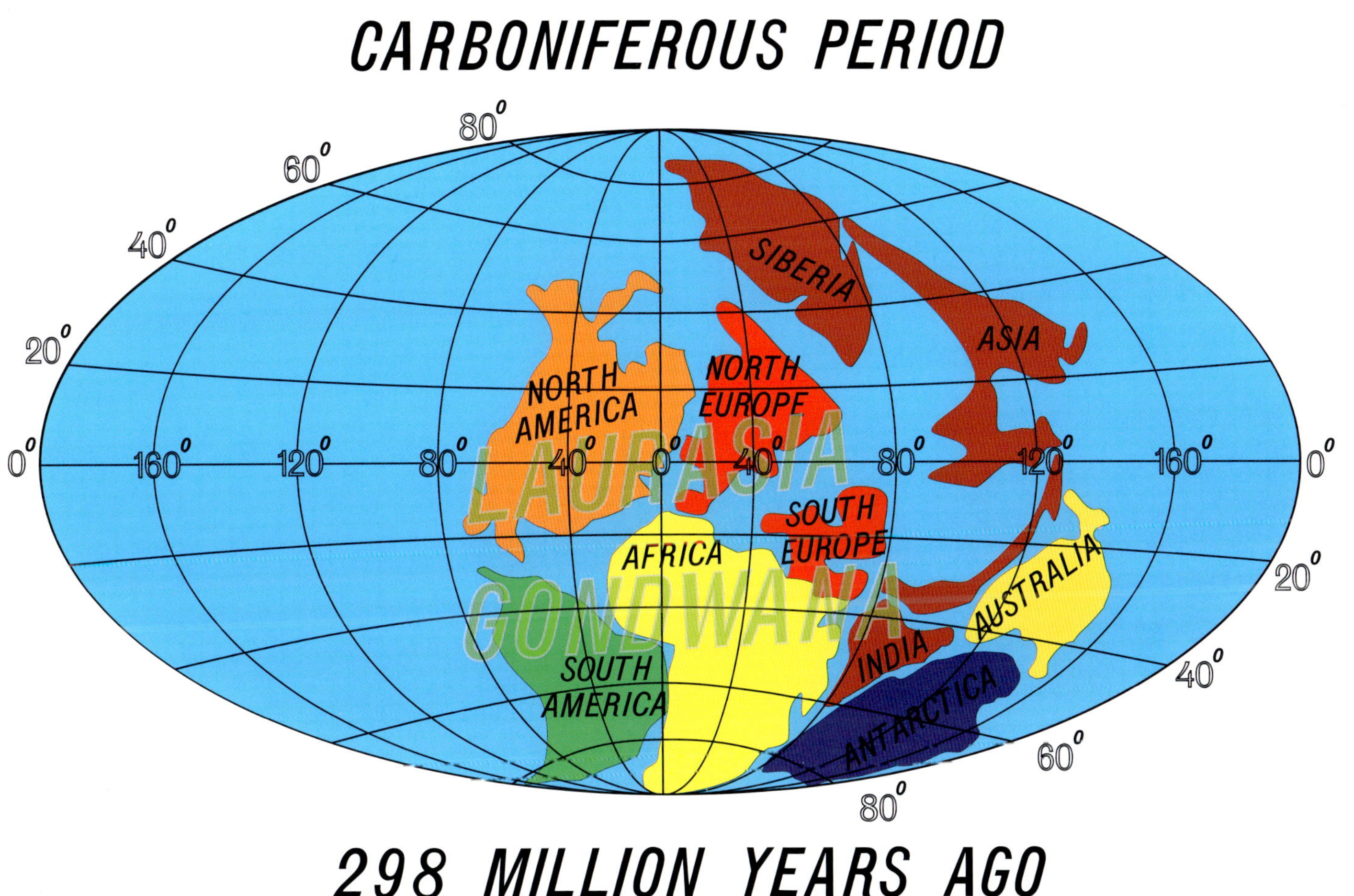

Greater Blue Mountains in New South Wales - This area has the largest range of different eucalypt trees found anywhere in the world. The Wollemi pine grows in remote parts of the Greater Blue Mountains. The ancestors of this 'living fossil' formed forests during the age of the dinosaurs.

Tasmanian Wilderness - The temperate wilderness in Tasmania covers 1.6 million hectares.

Wet Tropics of Queensland - The vegetation in these rainforests is scientifically important since it includes examples of nearly every stage of the development of plant life on Earth.

Fraser Island, Queensland - Although this is the largest sand island in the world, Fraser Island also has areas of tall rainforest.

Forests and Settlements in Australia

Clearing the Forests
Colonial settlers in Australia depended on forests. They cleared them to provide timber for building and to make space for housing, pastures and roads. The first settlements were mostly built in areas that had been covered with forests.

Burning the Forests
Once the trees had been cut down, settlers burned them. The first settlers had no tractors or other machinery to remove large tree stumps so they had to burn them. Some trees were too large to remove, so these were left to provide shade for livestock.

Wooden Fences
Cattle and sheep were brought to the early colonies on ships. Settlers built wooden fences to stop their valuable livestock escaping into the bush. Fences also discouraged theft.

Buildings
Timber from trees was the main building material for settlers' houses and sheds for their animals. Buildings made from bricks and stone were expensive and only wealthy people or the government had access to paid labourers or convicts to build them.

Food
Settlers hunted native forest animals for food and for sport. They were wary about eating the native plants, afraid that they might be poisonous.

Furniture
Furniture was expensive to import on ships, so a local furniture industry began very early in the history of settlement. The Australian red cedar was a prized timber and the items of furniture made from it in the 1800s are now rare antiques.

Convicts
The dense Australian forests were frightening places for the first settlers and only the most courageous convicts escaped from their guards and hid in the bush.

MAKE A CHOICE

Keep the forests or clear them to make room for people to live?

Which would you choose to do?

Bushfires

What Causes Bushfires

The risk of bushfires increases after periods of high rainfall, due to the extra plant growth that occurs. Bushfires in forests have both natural and human causes:

Settlers and Bushfires

Settlers were not used to the way bushfires spread and many died in huge bushfires in the 1800s. Old photographs of their tiny bark huts in the middle of a forest show how vulnerable to fire their homes were. Settlers used fire to clear the forest completely and create pastures for animals to graze on. This clearing took many years, even generations to complete. Settlers occasionally lost control of their fires and destructive bushfires resulted.

Bushfire Brigades

In Australia today, volunteer fire brigades fight bushfires. The NSW Rural Fire Service is the largest volunteer fire service in the world. It has over 2,000 brigades and 74,000 volunteers. Fire brigades undertake controlled burning, just as Australian Aboriginal people have been doing for thousands of years.

Residents in Fire-Prone Areas

Many people build their homes in forests across Australia, despite the risk of bushfires. They are prepared to take this risk to live somewhere so beautiful. Many local government bodies impose strict rules on the types of building that can be constructed in a fire-prone forest area. These rules govern the types of building materials that can be used and the style of the building. Residents in fire-prone areas are encouraged to have a fire plan so that each person knows what they have to do if a bushfire threatens them, their animals or their house. In rural areas, residents along a country road may have access to their own fire-fighting equipment that is stored in a location where they can hopefully reach it in an emergency.

Worst Recorded Bushfires in Australia

1926 - Gippsland Black Sunday fires in Victoria
1939 - Black Friday fires in Victoria
1967 - Black Tuesday fires in Tasmania
1983 - Ash Wednesday fires in Victoria and South Australia
1994 - Bushfires threatened Sydney suburbs
2009 - Black Saturday fires in Victoria

Forest Types in Australia

Eucalypt Forests

Location

Eucalypt forests comprise about 75 per cent of all Australian forests. Species of eucalypt trees grow in most areas except arid and alpine regions, but they need an annual rainfall of at least 500 mm to form forests.

Description

Eucalypt trees are commonly called gum trees. They form all types of forest, from dense closed forests to open woodland and mallee scrub.

Eucalypt trees survive in semi-arid areas by having thick, narrow leaves to help conserve water. Some depend on a bushfire for their seed pods to open. Their hard seeds survive the fire and then germinate once the fire has passed. Some eucalypts have buds under the soil from which regrowth occurs after a fire has destroyed the top of the tree. The high level of oil in eucalypt leaves makes the trees explode in flames during an intense bushfire.

Native Animals

Possums, wombats, wallabies, kookaburras, echidnas and many other animals recognised around the world as symbols of Australia all live in eucalypt forests. Koalas live in gum forests and eat only gum leaves. Since eucalypt forests make up three quarters of all the forests in Australia, they are the most common type of forest bordering suburban development. Because of this, the native animals of these forests frequently interact with humans.

Forest Animals as Pets?

It is unlawful to keep native forest animals as pets. What do you think is the reason for this?

Above: Forest with native camp & mia mia's, 1851

Aboriginal Australians and Eucalypt Forests

Aboriginal Australians invented many ways to use eucalypt trees:
Oil - medicine and healing
Sap - glue
Bark - canoes, containers, housing and cloaks
Timber - tools and weapons

Settlers and Eucalypt Forests

Early settlers cleared vast areas of eucalypt forest so they could plant crops and graze livestock on grasses. Most of the timber felled was burned in gigantic bonfires. While this behaviour would be unacceptable today, in the 1800s it was the only way settlers knew of to make use of the land. In some countries to the north of Australia, this mass burning of forests still occurs, resulting in a smoke haze that can be seen from space.

Eucalypt Forests and Economic Activity

- Eucalypt oil is used as a disinfectant, for cleaning and as a deodoriser.
- The timber industry uses many species of eucalypt trees, such as blackbutt, stringy bark, spotted gum, jarrah, mountain ash and blue gum.
- Eucalypt trees are grown in gardens across Australia's suburbs, where they make beautiful shade trees. They are also responsible for damage to property and injuries to people when they fall.
- Tourism in the eucalypt forests contributes to the economy and provides employment.
- Eucalypt trees have been exported to Africa and the USA to provide shade trees, timber and also for eucalypt oil.

Mallee Forests

Location

The largest mallee forests are located in the northwest of Victoria, in South Australia and in Western Australia. They grow in the semi-arid areas on the edges of deserts, or in the dry, sandy soils along the coast. There is a region called The Mallee, which is in South Australia and Victoria.

Description

The mallee is a eucalypt that has multiple small trunks and grows as a bush rather than a tall tree. They survive by having underground storage in their roots, which allows them to regrow after a bushfire or a drought. Leaves of mallee trees have waxy coverings, are not very large and hang vertically from branches. These are adaptations that reduce their water loss and exposure to sunlight. Seeds of mallee trees are hard and woody so they can survive a drought, even if the parent tree dies. The mallee trees provide shade and shelter for other plants that grow underneath them, including shrubs in wetter areas and grasses in semi-arid areas.

Native Animals

The mallee fowl builds a large mound as its nest. The female lays eggs in the mound and the male bird makes sure the temperature in the mound is perfect for incubating the chicks.

Other mallee forest animals include the mallee ringneck, the Major Mitchell's cockatoo and the tiny mallee emu-wren, which has a wispy tail.

Below: Mallee fowl

Above: Mallee tree in bloom
Right: Mallee trees

Aboriginal Australians and Mallee Forests

Mallee is an Aboriginal word meaning 'water'. Aboriginal Australians discovered that the tuber roots of mallee trees could be used as a source of water.

Settlers and Mallee Forests

European settlers found the mallee forests difficult to clear because of the dense root systems of the trees. The invention of the stump-jump plough made ploughing easier and larger areas could be used for agriculture. The intertwined roots provide good protection for rabbits and their burrows, so many mallee forests were destroyed as a way of dealing with the rabbit plague in the 19th and 20th centuries.

Mallee Forests and Economic Activity

- Brush fencing depends on the harvesting of mallee branches.
- Charcoal chicken shops traditionally use mallee charcoal because of the flavour it gives to the cooked chickens.
- Mallee charcoal is sold for home use in barbecues.

Threats to the Mallee Forests

- Feral animals and weeds
- Clearing
- Rising water table and increasing salinity of the ground water
- Overgrazing

Acacia Wattle Forests

Location

Various species of acacia grow throughout Australia in the non-desert areas. The most common types of acacia are mulga and brigalow. The largest acacia forests are in Western Australia where the climate is hot, dry and with low to moderate rainfall.

Description

Acacias can be shrubs or tall trees. They have thin leaves and yellow flowers and are commonly called wattles. The golden wattle is Australia's official floral emblem.

Aboriginal Australians and Acacia Forests

Acacia wood was used by Aboriginal Australians to make weapons and hunting tools such as the boomerang. The seeds of some species are a food, as is the sticky sap, and the roots can be roasted as a vegetable. Witchetty grubs live in acacia bark and have a nutty flavour when cooked.

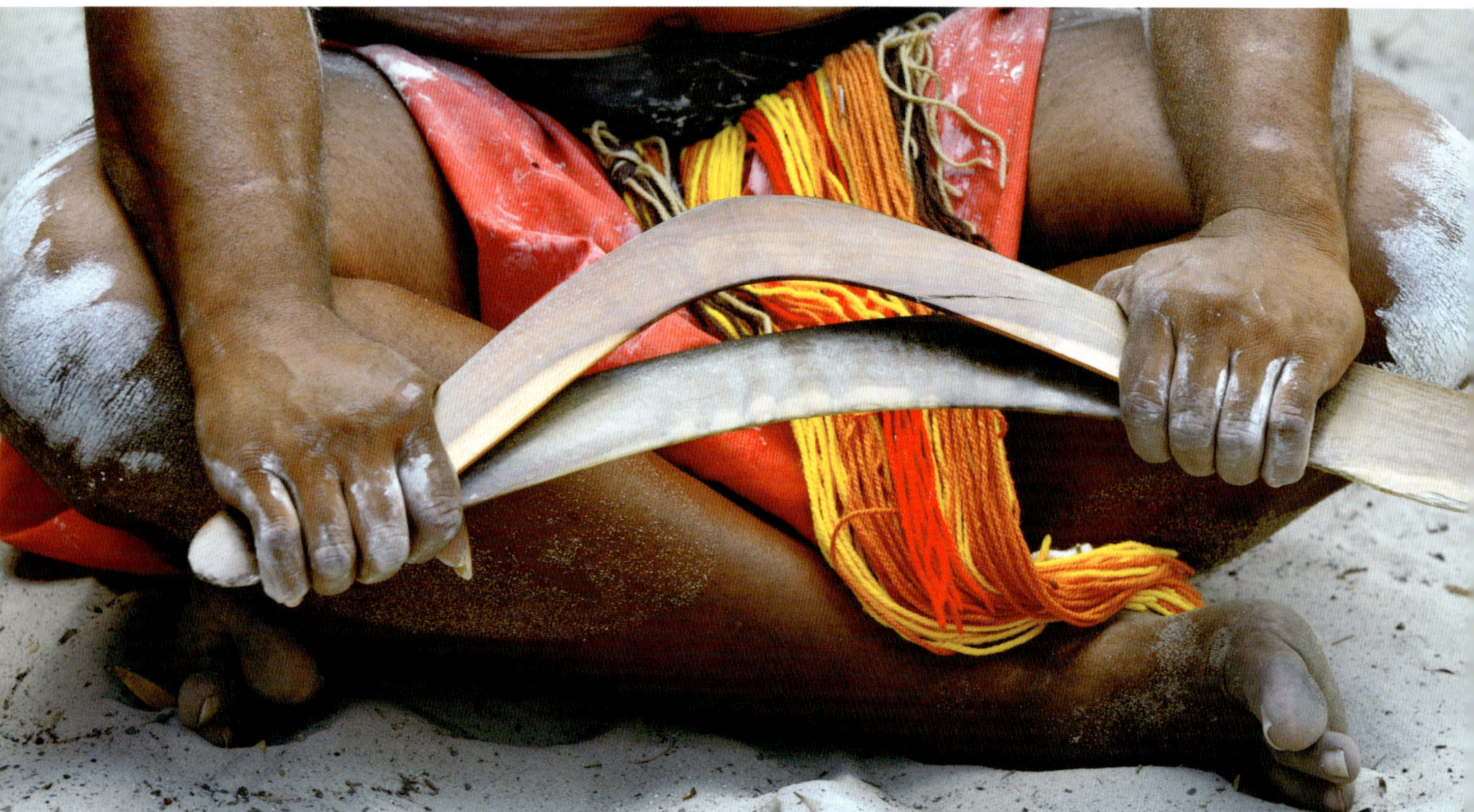

Acacia Forests and Economic Activity

- Farmers growing sandalwood also plant acacia trees to help enrich the soil. This happens when bacteria in the acacia roots leave nitrogen in the soil. The nitrogen helps the sandalwood trees grow.
- As in Australia, farmers in Africa and Indonesia also plant acacias to improve the soil.
- Some acacias provide food for sheep in times of drought.
- Early settlers used acacia wood to make furniture.

Inset: Witchetty grubs
Right: Acacia Wattle

Casuarina She-Oak Forests

Location
Casuarina trees grow in coastal and riverside locations. Most of the casuarina forests are in New South Wales and on Cape York.

Description
Although casuarinas are also called she-oaks, they are not related to oak trees. They produce little cones with seeds that are a food source for birds, such as the black cockatoo, and their leaves look like the long needles of pine trees. Casuarinas need a good water supply to grow.

Aboriginal Australians and Casuarina Forests
Aboriginal Australians used casuarina wood for boomerangs, weapons and shields.

Settlers and Casuarina Forests
Settlers used the casuarina wood to make roof shingles, fencing and farm tools.

Right: Casuarina Tree
Below: Black Cockatoo

NASA and Our Forests

Visit www.earthobervatory.nasa.gov

The NASA satellite images on this website show Australia's forests from space.

HANDY HINT
Try search terms such as 'forests Australia' or 'mangroves Australia'.

Mangrove Forests

Location

Mangrove trees grow in intertidal areas along the coast. They thrive in brackish conditions, which come from the mix between river water and saltwater from the ocean. Mangroves flourish in tropical and temperate climates. They do not grow in areas of extreme cold or where there is ice or snow.

Description

Mangroves are salt tolerant and can withstand being partly flooded by saltwater at high tide. Their aerial roots absorb oxygen from the air, and some mangroves can excrete excess salt through their leaves. Mangrove forests protect the land from erosion and from storm surges during cyclones. The large seeds float on water until they find a suitable place to grow.

Native Animals

Mangrove forests provide safe breeding areas for fish and other aquatic animals. Birds use the mangrove forests as nesting sites. The thick, intertwined mangrove roots, and the daily flooding with water from the tides, provide animals living amongst the mangroves with protection from land predators like dingoes or feral cats and dogs.

Take a Walk

Using the internet, research a mangrove forest and make a list of things you would see if you walked along a boardwalk there.

People and Mangrove Forests

People in Australia have settled mostly around the coasts and along rivers. These are also the habitats of mangroves. This has resulted in the removal of large areas of mangrove forests, as people sought to gain easier access to the water and to build harbours and wharves.

Mangrove forests were once thought of as disease-ridden swamps that had to be removed for the health and safety of human settlers. Unfortunately, this removal also destroyed the habitat of the creatures that rely on the mangroves. Prawns, barramundi and mud crabs all use mangrove forests as breeding sites, and the removal of mangroves diminishes their numbers. The largest natural predator in the mangroves is the crocodile, but human activity causes much more destruction. All around the coasts of Pacific region countries, mangroves are being removed and commercial fishing catches are reduced as a result.

The tourism industry has found that visitors enjoy exploring natural mangrove forests. Boardwalks built above the water level enable tourists to walk through the mangroves without having to wade in the water and mud.

Melaleuca Forests

Location

The largest melaleuca forests grow in northern Australia. The melaleuca forest on Cape York has remained largely untouched due to its remote location.

Description

Melaleuca trees have thick bark, which has many layers resembling thin sheets of paper. Although these trees prefer damp, swampy areas, gardeners around Australia manage to grow them as specimen trees. In swampy areas, the trees provide places for water birds to build their nests. The undergrowth, fallen branches and debris provide areas for aquatic creatures to breed when the ground is flooded by the tide or by overflowing creeks and rivers.

Aboriginal Australians and Melaleuca Forests

Australian Aboriginal people used the thin, papery bark of melaleuca trees as a traditional first aid treatment to cover wounds.

Settlers and Melaleuca Forests

- Melaleuca forests were once more widely spread around the swampy areas of Australia. As settlers filled in the swamps to provide riverside land for homes and businesses, the melaleuca trees that grew there disappeared.
- Agricultural practices that have increased the salt content of the soil adversely affect any nearby melaleuca trees.
- Melaleuca timber is water and termite resistant and has been logged to build structures that are permanently underwater, such as jetties.

Far right: White Melaleuca bush
Above: Paperbark
Left: Lorikeet feeding on red Melaleuca bush

SOMETHING TO THINK ABOUT

Tall, dense forests make up only 3% of the total forested area in Australia.

- What can we do to preserve these forests?
- Why is it important to do this?

Rainforests

Location

Although rainforests grow in areas with a high rainfall, they are not all the same. In temperate weather zones, such as in Tasmania, the forests have a dense canopy that reduces the amount of growth below on the ground. In sub-tropical climate zones, such as in northern Queensland, the rainforests are often referred to as jungles. These have a thick undergrowth of plants covering the forest floor.

Description

Rainforests cannot tolerate bushfires or regenerate like eucalypt forests. The plants have evolved to depend on moist, humid conditions and do not have adaptations for surviving bushfires.

Rainforests and the Atmosphere

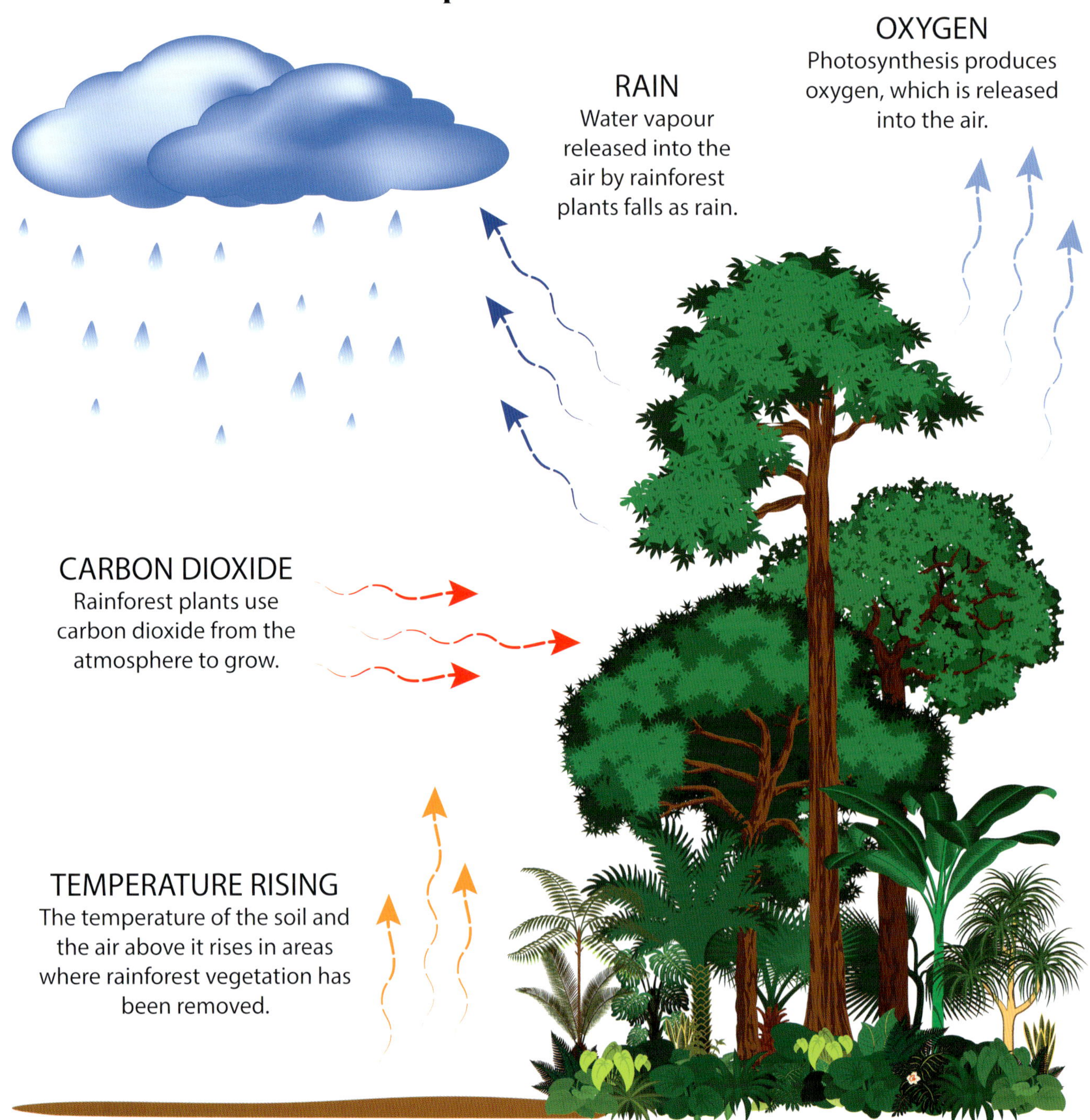

Rainforests and Economic Activity

- Ecotourism ventures in rainforests seek to provide visitors with comfortable facilities, while keeping the surroundings as natural as possible. Sewage, rubbish and building roads to resorts are the main challenges to the rainforest environments from ecotourism.
- Scientists believe that there are many rainforests plants that could contain chemicals that would benefit humans as medicines. The biodiversity of rainforests means that they probably harbour new species of plants and animals that have not yet been discovered or studied.
- Settlers have logged rainforest timbers since Europeans first arrived in Australia.

DID YOU KNOW?

In some children's textbooks in the mid 20th century, rainforest jungles were described as useless places that would be improved if there was logging to thin them out. This ill-informed idea grew from the notion held by many explorers and scientists in the 18th and 19th centuries that nature had to be of benefit to human beings for it to have any value.

Above: Hopetoun Falls

Gondwana

The ancient continent of Gondwana existed millions of years ago when the landmasses that are now Australia, India and New Guinea were all joined together. The descendants of some of the plants from that time are still alive in Australia's rainforests.

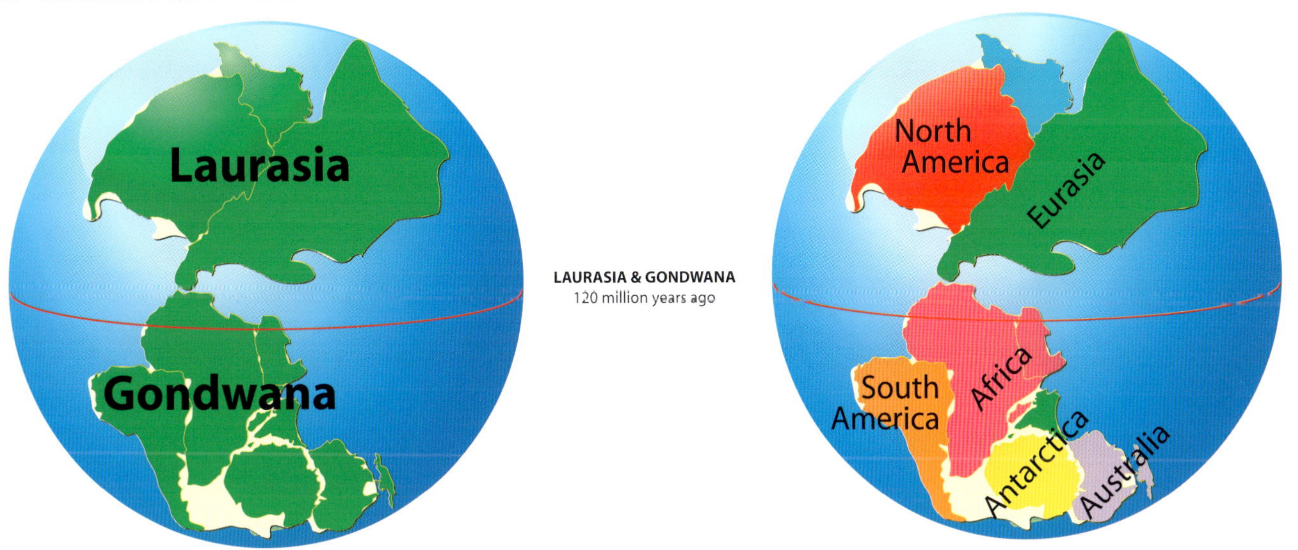

Sub-Alpine Forests

Location

The sub-alpine forests grow in high country and on mountainsides. Trees do not grow at the highest alpine areas, above about 1,800 metres high, where there are only grasses and shrubs. Sub-alpine forests grow in the Alpine National Park, which stretches from Victoria to the Kosciuszko National Park in New South Wales. At lower altitudes, the sub-alpine forest may merge with eucalypt forests and rainforests.

Description

Snow gums and mountain ash trees grow in sub-alpine areas and survive the snow and ice during winter. The undergrowth in these forests includes large areas of grass, which makes them a perfect location for wild brumbies to flourish. These horses are not native to Australia but are the descendants of those that were either released into the bush or escaped. Although they destroy the more delicate plant life in alpine and sub-alpine areas, many people believe the wild brumbies are iconic animals of the Australian high country.

Native animals have developed adaptations that allow them to survive in the cold, sub-alpine forests. Alpine dingoes have a thick coat to keep them warm. Leadbeater's Possum, Victoria's state animal emblem, lives in the hollows of mountain ash forest trees.

Right: Kosciuszko National Park
Below: Wild brumbies

DID YOU KNOW?

The sub-alpine forests are the locations written about in the poem The Man from Snowy River by Banjo Paterson. The wild brumbies mentioned in this poem still live in the sub-alpine forests.

Sub-Alpine Forests and Economic Activity

- Cattle have both a positive and negative effect on high country environments. Grazing in high country areas has caused damage to alpine plants, but the cattle also eat grasses that would otherwise provide fuel for bushfires.
- Tourism activities in the sub-alpine forests include skiing, camping, hunting, fishing, bushwalking and kayaking on the mountain streams.
- The ski industry draws tourists from around the world to resorts in New South Wales, Victoria and Tasmania Resort owners in these locations clear trees to make way for infrastructure and to provide safe ski runs.
- Settlers in the sub-alpine forests built huts from the timber they found around them. Today, the towns that service the ski fields have replaced the forests with shops, ski chalets, resorts and houses.

Callitris Conifer Forests

Location

Callitris trees grow mainly in eastern Australia and New Caledonia. They are the descendants of trees that grew on the ancient continent of Gondwana. Although there are a few locations where the callitris trees dominate in the forest, such as the north coast of New South Wales, it is more usual for these trees to grow together with eucalypts or wattles.

Description

Callitris trees are native conifers, which means they produce seeds in cones. They are sometimes called Cypress pines, although they are not related to pine trees. Callitris trees grow in sandy soils and they can tolerate a wide range of temperatures. Some callitris forests even exist on the edges of deserts. They cannot survive fires, so areas that experience severe and frequent bushfires do not offer a good environment for callitris. Some trees grow to fifty metres high.

Aboriginal Australians and Callitris Forests

- Callitris wood has been used by Aboriginal Australians for tools, weapons and musical instruments.
- Resin from the trees provided strong glue for attaching spearheads.
- The people of Arnhem Land use the bark to make belts.

Callitris Forests and Economic Activity

- Callitris wood is resistant to termites. It has been used for building, fences, furniture, telephone poles and floorboards.
- Callitris is the second most important native timber logged after eucalypt.
- Grazing occurs in the callitris forests.
- Oil from the native blue Cypress pine is used for aromatherapy.
- Resin is collected for varnishes and incense.

Plantation Forests

Plantation forests are grown in areas with a rainfall of at least 700 mm per year to avoid the need for expensive irrigation. These forests make up 8 per cent of all the forests in Australia.

Pine Plantations

Pine is a versatile timber used in building and carpentry. Small pine trees are also grown and sold each year as Christmas trees.

Sandalwood Plantations

Sandalwood has been grown in the Western Australian wheatbelt since colonial times when it was exported to Asia. Sandalwood needs to grow near other plants, such as casuarinas or wattles, which improve the nitrogen level in the soil. Sandalwood can only survive in areas that are not too wet or too dry. It is not processed in timber mills but is harvested in cut pieces instead, and both the fragrant wood and the nuts are a source of income for growers.

Eucalypt Plantations

Some eucalypt trees are harvested from native forests and some, such as blackbutt and blue gums, are grown in plantations.

Glossary

biome	habitat defined by its climate, plants and animals
brackish water	water having a low level of saltiness
certification	official approval by an organisation
crown	leafy top of a tree
emblem	symbol
germinate	start to grow
greenhouse gas	gas in the atmosphere that contributes to global warming
infrastructure	constructions needed for human activity
intertidal	area between high and low tides on the shore
NASA	The National Aeronautics and Space Administration
photosynthesis	chemical process used by plants to grow
resin	thick, sticky sap

Index

Visit this website to find out more about forests in Australia:
www.agriculture.gov.au/forestry/australias-forests